SONGS, MERRY AND SAD

SONGS

MERRY AND SAD

BY

JOHN CHARLES McNEILL

THE UNIVERSITY PRESS

CHAPEL HILL

TO

JOSEPH P. CALDWELL

("The Old Man")

Almost all these verses have been published before, a good many in The Century Magazine, some in The Youth's Companion, and the others in The Charlotte Observer. Thanks are due these periodicals for their courteous permission to republish.

CONTENTS

10

THE BRIDE

THE little white bride is left alone
With him, her lord; the guests have gone;
    The festal hall is dim.
No jesting now, nor answering mirth.
The hush of sleep falls on the earth
    And leaves her here with him.

Why should there be, O little white bride,
When the world has left you by his side,
    A tear to brim your eyes?
Some old love-face that comes again,
Some old love-moment sweet with pain
    Of passionate memories?

Does your heart yearn back with last regret
For the maiden meads of mignonette
    And the fairy-haunted wood,
That you had not withheld from love,
A little while, the freedom of
    Your happy maidenhood?

11

Or is it but a nameless fear,
A wordless joy, that calls the tear
      In dumb appeal to rise,
When, looking on him where he stands,
You yield up all into his hands,
      Pleading into his eyes?

For days that laugh or nights that weep
You two strike oars across the deep
      With life's tide at the brim;
And all time's beauty, all love's grace
Beams, little bride, upon your face
      Here, looking up at him.

"OH, ASK ME NOT"

Love, should I set my heart upon a crown,
    Squander my years, and gain it,
What recompense of pleasure could I own?
    For youth's red drops would stain it.

Much have I thought on what our lives may
        mean,
    And what their best endeavor,
Seeing we may not come again to glean,
    But, losing, lose forever.

Seeing how zealots, making choice of pain,
    From home and country parted,
Have thought it life to leave their fellows slain,
    Their women broken-hearted;

How teasing truth a thousand faces claims,
    As in a broken mirror,
And what a father died for in the flames
    His own son scorns as error;

13

How even they whose hearts were sweet with
    song
  Must quaff oblivion's potion,
And, soon or late, their sails be lost along
  The all-surrounding ocean:

Oh, ask me not the haven of our ships,
  Nor what flag floats above you!
I hold you close, I kiss your sweet, sweet lips,
  And love you, love you, love you!

ISABEL

WHEN first I stood before you,
    Isabel,
I stood there to adore you,
    In your spell;
For all that grace composes,
And all that beauty knows is
Your face above the roses,
    Isabel.

You knew the charm of flowers,
    Isabel,
Which, like incarnate hours,
    Rose and fell
At your bosom, glowed and gloried,
White and pale and pink and florid,
And you touched them with your forehead,
    Isabel.

Amid the jest and laughter,
    Isabel,
I saw you, and thereafter,
    Ill or well,

There was nothing else worth seeing,
Worth following or fleeing,
And no reason else for being,
      Isabel.

TO ———

SOME time, far hence, when Autumn sheds
    Her frost upon your hair,
And you together sit at dusk,
    May I come to you there?
And lightly will our hearts turn back
    To this, then distant, day
When, while the world was clad in flowers,
    You two were wed in May.

When we shall sit about your board
    Three old friends met again,
Joy will be with us, but not much
    Of jest and laughter then;
For Autumn's large content and calm,
    Like heaven's own smile, will bless
The harvest of your happy lives
    With store of happiness.

May you, who, flankt about with flowers,
    Will plight your faith to-day,
Hold, evermore enthroned, the love
    Which you have crowned in May;

17

And Time will sleep upon his scythe,
The swallow rest his wing,
Seeing that you at autumntide
Still clasp the hands of spring.

TO MELVIN GARDNER:

A FLIGHT of doves, with wanton wings,
   Flash white against the sky.
In the leafy copse an oriole sings,
   And a robin sings hard by.
Sun and shadow are out on the hills;
The swallow has followed the daffodils;
In leaf and blade, life throbs and thrills
   Through the wild, warm heart of May.

To have seen the sun come back, to have seen
   Children again at play,
To have heard the thrush where the woods are
     green
   Welcome the new-born day,
To have felt the soft grass cool to the feet,
To have smelt earth's incense, heavenly sweet,
To have shared the laughter along the street,
   And, then, to have died in May!

A thousand roses will blossom red,
    A thousand hearts be gay,
For the summer lingers just ahead
    And June is on her way;
The bee must bestir him to fill his cells,
The moon and the stars will weave new spells
Of love and the music of marriage bells—
    And, oh, to be dead in May!

AWAY DOWN HOME

'T WILL not be long before they hear
  The bullbat on the hill,
And in the valley through the dusk
  The pastoral whippoorwill.
A few more friendly suns will call
  The bluets through the loam
And star the lanes with buttercups
      Away down home.

"Knee-deep!" from reedy places
  Will sing the river frogs.
The terrapins will sun themselves
  On all the jutting logs.
The angler's cautious oar will leave
  A trail of drifting foam
Along the shady currents
      Away down home.

The mocking-bird will feel again
  The glory of his wings,
And wanton through the balmy air
  And sunshine while he sings,

With a new cadence in his call,
    The glint-wing'd crow will roam
From field to newly-furrowed field
        Away down home.

When dogwood blossoms mingle
    With the maple's modest red,
And sweet arbutus wakes at last
    From out her winter's bed,
'T would not seem strange at all to meet
    A dryad or a gnome,
Or Pan or Psyche in the woods
        Away down home.

Then come with me, thou weary heart!
    Forget thy brooding ills,
Since God has come to walk among
    His valleys and his hills!
The mart will never miss thee,
    Nor the scholar's dusty tome,
And the Mother waits to bless thee,
        Away down home.

FOR JANE'S BIRTHDAY

If fate had held a careless knife
   And clipped one line that drew,
Of all the myriad lines of life,
   From Eden up to you;
If, in the wars and wastes of time,
   One sire had met the sword,
One mother died before her prime
   Or wed some other lord;

Or had some other age been blest,
   Long past or yet to be,
And you had been the world's sweet guest
   Before or after me:
I wonder how this rose would seem,
   Or yonder hillside cot;
For, dear, I cannot even dream
   A world where you are not!

Thus heaven forfends that I shall drink
   The gall that might have been,
If aught had broken a single link
   Along the lists of men;

And heaven forgives me, whom it loves,
  For feigning such distress:
My heart is happiest when it proves
  Its depth of happiness.

Enough to see you where you are,
  Radiant with maiden mirth!
To bless whatever blessed star
  Presided o'er your birth,
That, on this immemorial morn,
  When heaven was bending low,
The gods were kind and you were born
  Twenty sweet years ago!

A SECRET

A LITTLE baby went to sleep
  One night in his white bed,
And the moon came by to take a peep
  At the little baby head.

A wind, as wandering winds will do,
  Brought to the baby there
Sweet smells from some quaint flower that grew
  Out on some hill somewhere.

And wind and flower and pale moonbeam
  About the baby's bed
Stirred and woke the funniest dream
  In the little sleepy head.

He thought he was all sorts of things
  From a lion to a cat;
Sometimes he thought he flew on **wings,**
  Or fell and fell, so that
25

When morning broke he was right glad
    But much surprised to see
Himself a soft, pink little lad
    Just like he used to be.

I would not give this story fame
    If there were room to doubt it,
But when he learned to talk, he came
    And told me all about it.

THE OLD BAD WOMAN

The Old Bad Woman was coming along,
Busily humming a sort of song.

You could barely see, below her bonnet,
Her chin where her long nose rested on it.

One tooth thrust out on her lower lip,
And she held one hand upon her hip.

Then we went to thinking mighty fast,
For we knew our time had come at last.

For what we had done and didn't do
The Old Bad Woman would put us through.

If you cried enough to fill your hat,
She wouldn't care; she was used to that.

Of the jam we had eaten, she would know;
How we ran barefooted in the snow;

27

How we cried when they made us take our bath;
How we tied the grass across the path;

How we bound together the cat and cur—
We couldn't deny these things to her.

She pulled her nose up off her chin
And blinked at us with an awful grin.

And we almost died, becaze and because
Her bony fingers looked like claws.

When she came on up to where we were,
How could we be polite to her?

You needn't guess how she put us through.
If you are bad, she'll visit you.

And when she leaves and hobbles off
You'll think that she has done enough;

For the Old Bad Woman will and can
Be just as bad as the Old Bad Man!

VALENTINE

THIS is the time for birds to mate;
    To-day the dove
Will mark the ancient amorous date
    With moans of love;
The crow will change his call to prate
    His hopes thereof.

The starling will display the red
    That lights his wings;
The wren will know the sweet things said
    By him who swings
And ducks and dips his crested head
    And sings and sings.

They are obedient to their blood,
    Nor ask a sign,
Save bouyant air and swelling bud,
    At hands divine,
But choose, each in the barren wood,
    His valentine.

In caution's maze they never wait
    Until they die;
They flock the season's open gate
    Ere time steals by.
Love, shall we see and imitate,
    You, love, and I?

A PHOTOGRAPH

WHEN in this room I turn in pondering pace
And find thine eyes upon me where I stand,
Led on, as by Enemo's silken strand,
I come and gaze and gaze upon thy face.

Framed round by silence, poised on pearl-white
     grace
Of curving throat, too sweet for beaded band,
It seems as if some wizard's magic wand
Had wrought thee for the love of all the race.

Dear face, that will not turn about to see
The tulips, glorying in the casement sun,
Or, other days, the drizzled raindrops run

Down the damp walls, but follow only me,
Would that Pygmalion's goddess might be won
To change this lifeless image into thee!

JESSE COVINGTON

If I have had some merry times
    In roaming up and down the earth,
Have made some happy-hearted rhymes
    And had my brimming share of mirth,
And if this song should live in fame
    When my brief day is dead and gone,
Let it recall with mine the name
    Of old man Jesse Covington.

Let it recall his waggish heart—
    Yeke-hey, yeke-hey, hey-diddle-diddle—
When, while the fire-logs fell apart,
    He snatched the bow across his fiddle,
And looked on, with his eyes half shut,
    Which meant his soul was wild with fun,
At our mad capers through the hut
    Of old man Jesse Covington.

For all the thrilling tales he told,
    For all the tunes the fiddle knew,
For all the glorious nights of old
    We boys and he have rollicked through,

32

For laughter all unknown to wealth
   That roared responsive to a pun,
A hale, ripe age and ruddy health
   To old man Jesse Covington!

AN IDYL

Upon a gnarly, knotty limb
  That fought the current's crest,
Where shocks of reeds peeped o'er the brim,
  Wild wasps had glued their nest.

And in a sprawling cypress' grot,
  Sheltered and safe from flood,
Dirt-daubers each had chosen a spot
  To shape his house of mud-

In a warm crevice of the bark
  A basking scorpion clung,
With bright blue tail and red-rimmed eyes
  And yellow, twinkling tongue.

A lunging trout flashed in the sun,
  To do some petty slaughter,
And set the spiders all a-run
  On little stilts of water.

34

Toward noon upon the swamp there stole
   A deep, cathedral hush,
Save where, from sun-splocht bough and bole,
   Sweet thrush replied to thrush.

An angler came to cast his fly
   Beneath a baffling tree.
I smiled, when I had caught his eye,
   And he smiled back at me.

When stretched beside a shady elm
   I watched the dozy heat,
Nature was moving in her realm,
   For I could hear her feet.

HOME SONGS

The little loves and sorrows are my song:
　　The leafy lanes and birthsteads of my sires,
　　Where memory broods by winter's evening
　　　　fires
O'er oft-told joys, and ghosts of ancient
　　　　wrong;
The little cares and carols that belong
　　To home-hearts, and old rustic lutes and
　　　　lyres,
　　And spreading acres, where calm-eyed desires
Wake with the dawn, unfevered, fair, and
　　　　strong.

If words of mine might lull the bairn to sleep,
　　And tell the meaning in a mother's eyes;
Might counsel love, and teach their eyes to weep
　　Who, o'er their dead, question unanswering
　　　　skies,
More worth than legions in the dust of strife,
Time, looking back at last, should count my life.

36

M. W. RANSOM

(Died October 8, 1904)

For him, who in a hundred battles stood
    Scorning the cannon's mouth,
Grimy with flame and red with foeman's blood,
    For thy sweet sake, O South;

Who, wise as brave, yielded his conquered sword
    At a vain war's surcease,
And spoke, thy champion still, the statesman's
        word
    In the calm halls of peace;

Who pressed the ruddy wine to thy faint lips,
    Where thy torn body lay,
And saw afar time's white in-sailing ships
    Bringing a happier day:

Oh, mourn for him, dear land that gave him
        birth!
    Bow low thy sorrowing head!
Let thy seared leaves fall silent on the earth
    Whereunder he lies dead!

In field and hall, in valor and in grace,
    In wisdom's livery,
Gentle and brave, he moved with knightly pace,
    A worthy son of thee!

PROTEST

Oh, I am weary, weary, weary
   Of Pan and oaten quills
And little songs that, from the dictionary,
   Learn lore of streams and hills,
Of studied laughter, mocking what is merry,
   And calculated thrills!

Are we grown old and past the time of singing?
   Is ardor quenched in art
Till art is but a formal figure, bringing
   A money-measured heart,
Procrustean cut, and, with old echoes, ringing
   Its bells about the mart?

The race moves on, and leaves no wildernesses
   Where rugged voices cry;
It reads its prayer, and with set phrase it
     blesses
   The souls of men who die,
And step by even step its rank progresses,
   An army marshalled by.

If it be better so, that Babel noises,
    Losing all course and ken,
And grief that wails and gladness that rejoices
    Should never wake again
To shock a world of modulated voices
    And mediocre men,

Then he is blest who wears the painted feather
    And may not turn about
To dusks when muses romped the dewy heather
    In unrestricted rout
And dawns when, if the stars had sung together,
    The sons of God would shout!

OBLIVION

Green moss will creep
Along the shady graves where we shall sleep.

Each year will bring
Another brood of birds to nest and sing.

At dawn will go
New ploughmen to the fields we used to know.

Night will call home
The hunter from the hills we loved to roam.

She will not ask,
The milkmaid, singing softly at her task,

Nor will she care
To know if I were brave or you were fair.

No one will think
What chalice life had offered us to drink,

When from our clay
The sun comes back to kiss the snow away.

41

NOW!

HER brown hair knew no royal crest,
   No gems nor jeweled charms,
No roses her bright cheek caressed,
   No lilies kissed her arms.
In simple, modest womanhood
   Clad, as was meet, in white,
The fairest flower of all, she stood
   Amid the softest light.

It had been worth a perilous quest
   To see the court she drew,—
My rose, my gem, my royal crest,
   My lily moist with dew;
Worth heaven, when, with farewells from each,
   The gay throng let us be,
To see her turn at last and reach
   Her white hands out to me.

TOMMY SMITH

WHEN summer's languor drugs my veins
  And fills with sleep the droning times,
Like sluggish dreams among my brains,
  There runs the drollest sort of rhymes,
Idle as clouds that stray through heaven
  And vague as if they were a myth,
But in these rhymes is always given
  A health for old Bluebritches Smith.

Among my thoughts of what is good
  In olden times and distant lands,
Is that do-nothing neighborhood
  Where the old cider-hogshead stands
To welcome with its brimming gourd
  The canny crowd of kin and kith
Who meet about the bibulous board
  Of old Bluebritches Tommy Smith.

In years to come, when stealthy change
  Hath stolen the cider-press away

43

And the gnarled orchards of the grange
   Have fallen before a slow decay,
Were I so cunning, I would carve
   From some time-scorning monolith
A sculpture that should well preserve
   The fame of old Bluebritches Smith.

BEFORE BEDTIME

THE cat sleeps in a chimney jam
   With ashes in her fur,
An' Tige, from on the yuther side,
   He keeps his eye on her.

The jar o' curds is on the hearth,
   An' I'm the one to turn it.
I'll crawl in bed an' go to sleep
   When maw begins to churn it.

Paw bends to read his almanax
   An' study out the weather,
An' bud has got a gourd o' grease
   To ile his harness leather.

Sis looks an' looks into the fire,
   Half-squintin' through her lashes,
An' I jis watch my tater where
   It shoots smoke through the ashes.

"IF I COULD GLIMPSE HIM"

When in the Scorpion circles low
   The sun with fainter, dreamier light,
And at a far-off hint of snow
   The giddy swallows take to flight,
And droning insects sadly know
   That cooler falls the autumn night;

When airs breathe drowsily and sweet,
   Charming the woods to colors gay,
And distant pastures send the bleat
   Of hungry lambs at break of day,
Old Hermes' wings grow on my feet,
   And, good-by, home! I'm called away!

There on the hills should I behold,
   Sitting upon an old gray stone
That humps its back up through the mold,
   And piping in a monotone,
Pan, as he sat in days of old,
   My joy would bid surprise begone!

46

Dear Pan! 'Tis he that calls me out;
  He, lying in some hazel copse,
Where lazily he turns about
  And munches each nut as it drops,
Well pleased to see me swamped in doubt
  At sound of his much-changing stops.

If I could glimpse him by the vine
  Where purple fox-grapes hang their store,
I'd tell him, in his leafy shrine,
  How poets say he lives no more.
He'd laugh, and pluck a muscadine,
  And fall to piping, as of yore!

ATTRACTION

He who wills life wills its condition sweet,
Having made love its mother, joy its quest,
That its perpetual sequence might not rest
On reason's dictum, cold and too discreet;

For reason moves with cautious, careful feet,
Debating whether life or death were best,
And why pale pain, not ruddy mirth, is guest
In many a heart which life hath set to beat.

But I will cast my fate with love, and trust
Her honeyed heart that guides the pollened bee
And sets the happy wing-seeds fluttering free;

And I will bless the law which saith, Thou must!
And, wet with sea or shod with weary dust,
Will follow back and back and back to thee!

LOVE'S FASHION

Oh, I can jest with Margaret
    And laugh a gay good-night,
But when I take my Helen's hand
    I dare not clasp it tight.

I dare not hold her dear white hand
    More than a quivering space,
And I should bless a breeze that blew
    Her hair into my face.

'T is Margaret I call sweet names:
    Helen is too, too dear
For me to stammer little words
    Of love into her ear.

So now, good-night, fair Margaret,
    And kiss me e'er we part!
But one dumb touch of Helen's hand,
    And, oh, my heart, my heart!

ALCESTIS

Not long the living weep above their dead,
And you will grieve, Admetus, but not long.
The winter's silence in these desolate halls
Will break with April's laughter on your lips;
The bees among the flowers, the birds that mate,
The widowed year, grown gaunt with memory
And yearning toward the summer's fruits, will
    come
With lotus comfort, feeding all your veins.
The vining brier will crawl across my grave,
And you will woo another in my stead.
Those tender, foolish names you called me by,
Your passionate kiss that clung unsatisfied,
The pressure of your hand, when dark night
    hushed
Life's busy stir, and left us two alone,
Will you remember? or, when dawn creeps in,
And you bend o'er another's pillowed head,
Seeing sleep's loosened hair about her face,
Until her low love-laughter welcomes you,

Will you, down-gazing at her waking eyes,
Forget?
         So have I loved you, my Admetus,
I thank the cruel fates who clip my life
To lengthen yours, they tarry not for age
To dim my eye and blanch my cheek, but now
Take me, while my lips are sweet to you
And youth hides yet amid this hair of mine,
Brown in the shadow, golden in the light.
Bend down and kiss me, dying for your sake,
Not gratefully, but sadly, love's farewell;
And if the flowering year's oblivion
Lend a new passion to thy life, far down
In the dim Stygian shadows wandering,
I will not know, but still will cherish there,
Where no change comes, thy love upon my lips.

REMINISCENCE

We sang old love-songs on the way
   In sad and merry snatches,
Your fingers o'er the strings astray
   Strumming the random catches.

And ever, as the skiff plied on
   Among the trailing willows,
Trekking the darker deeps to shun
   The gleaming sandy shallows,

It seemed that we had, ages gone,
   In some far summer weather,
When this same faery moonlight shone,
   Sung these same songs together.

And every grassy cape we passed,
   And every reedy island,
Even the bank'd cloud in the west
   That loomed a sombre highland;

And you, with dewmist on your hair,
  Crowned with a wreath of lilies,
Laughing like Lalage the fair
  And tender-eyed like Phyllis:

I know not if 't were here at home,
  By some old wizard's orders,
Or long ago in Crete or Rome
  Or fair Provençal borders,

But now, as when a faint flame breaks
  From out its smouldering embers,
My heart stirs in its sleep, and wakes,
  And yet but half-remembers

That you and I some other time
  Moved through this dream of glory,
Like lovers in an ancient rhyme,
  A long-forgotten story.

SONNET

I WOULD that love were subject unto law!
　　Upon his person I should lay distraint
　　And force him thus to answer my complaint,
Which I, in well-considered counts, should draw.
Not free to fly, he needs must seek some flaw
　　　　To mar my pleading, though his heart were
　　　　　　faint;
　　Declare his counsel to me, and acquaint
Himself with maxim, precedent, and saw.

Ah, I could win him with authorities,
　　If suing thus in such a sober court;
　　Could read him many an ancient rhym'd re-
　　　　port
Of such sad cases, tears would fill his eyes
　　And he confess a judgment, or resort
To some well-pleasing terms of compromise!

LINES

To you, dear mother heart, whose hair is **gray**
Above this page to-day,
Whose face, though lined with many a smile
    and care,
Grows year by year more fair,

Be tenderest tribute set in perfect rhyme,
That haply passing time
May cull and keep it for strange lips to pay
When we have gone our way;

And, to strange men, weary of field and street,
Should this, my song, seem sweet,
Yours be the joy, for all that made it so
You know, dear heart, you know.

AN EASTER HYMN

THE Sun has come again and fed
  The lily's lamp with light,
And raised from dust a rose, rich red,
  And a little star-flower, white;
He also guards the Pleiades
  And holds his planets true:
But we—we know not which of these
  The easier task to do.

But, since from heaven he stoops to breathe
  A flower to balmy air,
Surely our lives are not beneath
  The kindness of his care;
And, as he guides the blade that gropes
  Up from the barren sod,
So, from the ashes of our hopes,
  Will beauty grow toward God.

Whate'er thy name, O Soul of Life,—
  We know but that thou art,—

56

Thou seest, through all our waste of strife,
  One groping human heart,
Weary of words and broken sight,
  But moved with deep accord
To worship where thy lilies light
  The altar of its Lord.

A CHRISTMAS HYMN

Near where the shepherds watched by night
  And heard the angels o'er them,
The wise men saw the starry light
  Stand still at last before them.
No armored castle there to ward
  His precious life from danger,
But, wrapped in common cloth, our Lord
  Lay in a lowly manger.
No booming bells proclaimed his birth,
  No armies marshalled by,
No iron thunders shook the earth,
  No rockets clomb the sky;
The temples builded in his name
  Were shapeless granite then,
And all the choirs that sang his fame
  Were later breeds of men.
But, while the world about him slept,
  Nor cared that he was born,
One gentle face above him kept
  Its mother watch till morn;

And, if his baby eyes could tell
　　What grace and glory were,
No roar of gun, no boom of bell
　　Were worth the look of her.
Now praise to God that ere his grace
　　Was scorned and he reviled
He looked into his mother's face,
　　A little helpless child;
And praise to God that ere men strove
　　About his tomb in war
One loved him with a mother's love,
　　Nor knew a creed therefor.

WHEN I GO HOME

When I go home, green, green will glow the
    grass,
Whereon the flight of sun and cloud will pass;
    Long lines of wood-ducks through the deep-
      ening gloam
Will hold above the west, as wrought on brass,
    And fragrant furrows will have delved the
      loam,
          When I go home.

When I go home, the dogwood stars will dash
The solemn woods above the bearded ash,
    The yellow-jasmine, whence its vine hath
      clomb,
Will blaze the valleys with its golden flash,
    And every orchard flaunt its polychrome,
          When I go home.

When I go home and stroll about the farm,
The thicket and the barnyard will be warm.

Jess will be there, and Nigger Bill, and
    Tom—
On whom time's chisel works no hint of harm—
And, oh, 'twill be a day to rest and roam,
    When I go home!

ODESSA

A HORROR of great darkness over them,
No cloud of fire to guide and cover them,
Beasts for the shambles, tremulous with dread,
They crouch on alien soil among their dead.

"Thy shield and thy exceeding great reward,"
This was thine ancient covenant, O Lord,
Which, sealed with mirth, these many thousand
    years
Is black with blood and blotted out with tears.

Have these not toiled through Egypt's burning
    sun,
And wept beside the streams of Babylon,
Led from thy wilderness of hill and glen
Into a wider wilderness of men?

Life bore them ever less of gain than loss,
Before and since Golgotha's piteous Cross,
And surely, now, their sorrow hath sufficed
For all the hate that grew from love of Christ!

Thou great God-heart, heed thou thy people's
    cry,
Bare-browed and empty-handed where they die,
Sea-sundered from wall-girt Jerusalem,
There being no sword that wills to succor
    them,—

And Miriam's song, long hushed, will rise to
    thee,
And all thy people lift their eyes to thee,
When, for the darkness' horror over them,
Thou comest, a cloud of light to cover them.

TRIFLES

WHAT shall I bring you, sweet?
  A posy prankt with every April hue:
  The cloud-white daisy, violet sky-blue,
  Shot with the primrose sunshine through and
      through?

Or shall I bring you, sweet,
  Some ancient rhyme of lovers sore beset,
  Whose joy is dead, whose sadness lingers yet,
  That you may read, and sigh, and soon for-
      get?

What shall I bring you, sweet?
  Was ever trifle yet so held amiss
  As not to fill love's waiting heart with bliss,
  And merit dalliance at a long, long kiss?

SUNBURNT BOYS

Down on the Lumbee river
  Where the eddies ripple cool
Your boat, I know, glides stealthily
  About some shady pool.
The summer's heats have lulled asleep
  The fish-hawk's chattering noise,
And all the swamp lies hushed about
  You sunburnt boys.

You see the minnow's waves that rock
  The cradled lily leaves.
From a far field some farmer's song,
  Singing among his sheaves,
Comes mellow to you where you sit,
  Each man with boatman's poise,
There, in the shimmering water lights,
  You sunburnt boys.

I know your haunts: each gnarly bole
  That guards the waterside,

Each tuft of flags and rushes where
    The river reptiles hide,
Each dimpling nook wherein the bass
    His eager life employs
Until he dies—the captive of
    You sunburnt boys.

You will not—will you?—soon forget
    When I was one of you,
Nor love me less that time has borne
    My craft to currents new;
Nor shall I ever cease to share
    Your hardships and your joys,
Robust, rough-spoken, gentle-hearted
    Sunburnt boys!

GRAY DAYS

A SOAKING sedge,
A faded field, a leafless hill and hedge,

Low clouds and rain,
And loneliness and languor worse than pain.

Mottled with moss,
Each gravestone holds to heaven a patient
    Cross.

Shrill streaks of light
Two sycamores' clean-limbed, funereal white,

And low between,
The sombre cedar and the ivy green.

Upon the stone
Of each in turn who called this land his own

The gray rain beats
And wraps the wet world in its flying sheets,

And at my eaves
A slow wind, ghostlike, comes and grieves and
    grieves.

AN INVALID

I CARE not what his name for God may be,
   Nor what his wisdom holds of heaven and
      hell,
   The alphabet whereby he strives to spell
His lines of life, nor where he bends his knee,
Since, with his grave before him, he can see
   White Peace above it, while the churchyard
      bell
   Poised in its tower, poised now, to boom his
      knell,
Seems but the waiting tongue of liberty.

For names and knowledge, idle breed of breath,
   And cant and creed, the progeny of strife,
   Thronging the safe, companioned streets of
      life,
Shrink trembling from the cold, clear eye of
      death,
   And learn too late why dying lips can smile:
   That goodness is the only creed worth while.

A CAGED MOCKING-BIRD

I PASS a cobbler's shop along the street
   And pause a moment at the door-step, where,
In nature's medley, piping cool and sweet,
    The songs that thrill the swamps when spring
      is near,
   Fly o'er the fields at fullness of the year,
And twitter where the autumn hedges run,
Join all the months of music into one.

I shut my eyes: the shy wood-thrush is there,
   And all the leaves hang still to catch his spell;
Wrens cheep among the bushes; from some-
      where
    A bluebird's tweedle passes o'er the fell;
    From rustling corn bob-white his name doth
      tell;
And when the oriole sets his full heart free
Barefooted boyhood comes again to me.

The vision-bringer hangs upon a nail
   Before a dusty window, looking dim

On marts where trade goes hot with box and
   bale;
   The sad-eyed passers have no time for him.
   His captor sits, with beaded face and grim,
Plying a listless awl, as in a dream
Of pastures winding by a shady stream.

Gray bird, what spirit bides with thee unseen?
   For now, when every songster finds his love
And makes his nest where woods are deep and
         green,
      Free as the winds, thy song should mock the
         dove.
      If I were thou, my grief in moans should
         move
At thinking—otherwhere, by others' art
Charmed and forgetful—of mine own sweet-
         heart.

But I, who weep when fortune seems unkind
   To prison me within a space of walls,
When far-off grottoes hold my loves enshrined
   And every love is cruel when it calls;
      Who sulk for hills and fern-fledged water-
         falls,—
I blush to offer sorrow unto thee,
Master of fate, scorner of destiny!

70

DAWN

THE hills again reach skyward with a smile.
  Again, with waking life along its way,
The landscape marches westward mile on mile
  And time throbs white into another day.

Though eager life must wait on livelihood,
  And all our hopes be tethered to the mart,
Lacking the eagle's wild, high freedom, would
  That ours might be this day the eagle's heart!

HARVEST

Cows in the stall and sheep in the fold;
Clouds in the west, deep crimson and gold;
  A heron's far flight to a roost somewhere;
  The twitter of killdees keen in the air;
The noise of a wagon that jolts through the
    gloam
        On the last load home.

There are lights in the windows; a blue spire of
    smoke
Climbs from the grange grove of elm and oak.
  The smell of the Earth, where the night pours
    to her
  Its dewy libation, is sweeter than myrrh,
And an incense to Toil is the smell of the loam
        On the last load home.

TWO PICTURES

ONE sits in soft light, where the hearth is warm,
    A halo, like an angel's, on her hair.
She clasps a sleeping infant in her arm.
    A holy presence hovers round her there,
    And she, for all her mother-pains more fair,
Is happy, seeing that all sweet thoughts that
        stir
The hearts of men bear worship unto her.

Another wanders where the cold wind blows,
    Wet-haired, with eyes that sting one like a
        knife.
Homeless forever, at her bosom close
    She holds the purchase of her love and life,
    Of motherhood, unglorified as wife;
And bitterer than the world's relentless scorn
The knowing her child were happier never born.

Whence are the halo and the fiery shame
    That fashion thus a crown and curse of love?

Have roted words such power to bless and
    blame?
  Ay, men have stained a raven from many a
    dove,
  And all the grace and all the grief hereof
Are the two words which bore one's lips apart
And which the other hoarded in her heart.

He who stooped down and wrote upon the sand,
  The God-heart in him touched to tenderness,
Saw deep, saw what we cannot understand,—
  We, who draw near the shrine of one to bless
  The while we scourge another's sore distress,
And judge like gods between the ill and good,
The glory and the guilt of womanhood.

OCTOBER

THE thought of old, dear things is in thine
    eyes,
O, month of memories!
Musing on days thine heart hath sorrow of,
Old joy, dead hope, dear love,

I see thee stand where all thy sisters meet
To cast down at thy feet
The garnered largess of the fruitful year,
And on thy cheek a tear.

Thy glory flames in every blade and leaf
To blind the eyes of grief;
Thy vineyards and thine orchards bend with
    fruit
That sorrow may be mute;

A hectic splendor lights thy days to sleep,
Ere the gray dusk may creep
Sober and sad along thy dusty ways,
Like a lone nun, who prays;

High and faint-heard thy passing migrant
    calls;
Thy lazy lizard sprawls
On his gray stone, and many slow winds creep
About thy hedge, asleep;

The sun swings farther toward his love, the
    south,
To kiss her glowing mouth;
And Death, who steals among thy purpling
    bowers,
Is deeply hid in flowers.

Would that thy streams were Lethe, and might
    flow
Where lotus blossoms blow,
And all the sweets wherewith thy riches bless
Might hold no bitterness!

Would, in thy beauty, we might all forget
Dead days and old regret,
And through thy realm might fare us forth to
    roam,
Having no thought for home!

And yet I feel, beneath thy queen's attire,
Woven of blood and fire,
Beneath the golden glory of thy charm
Thy mother heart beats warm,

76

And if, mayhap, a wandering child of thee,
Weary of land and sea,
Should turn him homeward from his dreamer's
    quest
To sob upon thy breast,

Thine arm would fold him tenderly, to prove
How thine eyes brimmed with love,
And thy dear hand, with all a mother's care,
Would rest upon his hair.

THE OLD CLOCK

ALL day low clouds and slanting rain
Have swept the woods and dimmed the plain.
Wet winds have swayed the birch and oak,
And caught and swirled away the smoke,
But, all day long, the wooden clock
   Went on, Nic-noc, nic-noc.

When deep at night I wake with fear,
And shudder in the dark to hear
The roaring storm's unguided strength,
Peace steals into my heart at length,
When, calm amid the shout and shock,
   I hear, Nic-noc, nic-noc.

And all the winter long 't is I
Who bless its sheer monotony—
Its scorn of days, which cares no whit
For time, except to measure it:
The prosy, dozy, cosy clock,
   Nic-noc, nic-noc, nic-noc!

TEAR STAINS

Tear-marks stain from page to page
  This book my fathers left to me,—
So dull that nothing but its age
  Were worth its freight across the sea.

But tear stains! When, by whom, and why?
  Thus takes my fancy to its wings;
For grief is old, and one may cry
  About so many things!

A PRAYER

IF many years should dim my inward sight,
  'Till, stirred with no emotion,
I might stand gazing at the fall of night
  Across the gloaming ocean;

Till storm, and sun, and night, vast with her
    stars,
  Would seem an oft-told story,
And the old sorrow of heroic wars
  Be faded of its glory;

Till, hearing, while June's roses blew their
    musk,
  The noise of field and city,
The human struggle, sinking tired at dusk,
  I felt no thrill of pity;

Till dawn should come without her old desire,
  And day brood o'er her stages,—
O let me die, too frail for nature's hire,
  And rest a million ages.

SHE BEING YOUNG

THE home of love is her blue eyes,
Wherein all joy, all beauty lies,
More sweet than hopes of paradise,
    She being young.

Speak of her with a miser's praise;
She craves no golden speech; her ways
Wind through charmed nights and magic days,
    She being young.

She is so far from pain and death,
So warm her cheek, so sweet her breath
Glad words are all the words she saith,
    She being young.

Seeing her face, it seems not far
To Troy's heroic field of war,
To Troy and all great things that are,
    She being young.

PAUL JONES

A century of silent suns
   Have set since he was laid on sleep,
And now they bear with booming guns
   And streaming banners o'er the deep
A withered skin and clammy hair
   Upon a frame of human bones:
Whose corse? We neither know nor care,
   Content to name it John Paul Jones.

His dust were as another's dust;
   His bones—what boots it where they lie?
What matter where his sword is rust,
   Or where, now dark, his eagle eye?
No foe need fear his arm again,
   Nor love, nor praise can make him whole;
But o'er the farthest sons of men
   Will brood the glory of his soul.

Careless though cenotaph or tomb
   Shall tower his country's monument,

Let banners float and cannon boom,
    A million-throated shout be spent,
Until his widowed sea shall laugh
    With sunlight in her mantling foam,
While, to his tomb or cenotaph,
    We bid our hero welcome home.

Twice exiled, let his ashes rest
    At home, afar, or in the wave,
But keep his great heart with us, lest
    Our nation's greatness find its grave;
And, while the vast deep listens by,
    When armored wrong makes terms to right,
Keep on our lips his proud reply,
    "Sir, I have but begun to fight!"

THE DRUDGE

Repose upon her soulless face,
   Dig the grave and leave her;
But breathe a prayer that, in his grace,
He who so loved this toiling race
   To endless rest receive her.

Oh, can it be the gates ajar
   Wait not her humble quest,
Whose life was but a patient war
Against the death that stalked from far
   With neither haste nor rest;

To whom were sun and moon and cloud,
   The streamlet's pebbly coil,
The transient, May-bound, feathered crowd,
The storm's frank fury, thunder-browed,
   But witness of her toil;

Whose weary feet knew not the bliss
   Of dance by jocund reed;
Who never dallied at a kiss!
If heaven refuses her, life is
   A tragedy indeed!

THE WIFE

THEY locked him in a prison cell,
 Murky and mean.
She kissed him there a wife's farewell
 The bars between.
And when she turned to go, the crowd,
Thinking to see her shamed and bowed,
Saw her pass out as calm and proud
 As any queen.

She passed a kinsman on the street,
 To whose sad eyes
She made reply with smile as sweet
 As April skies.
To one who loved her once and knew
The sorrow of her life, she threw
A gay word, ere his tale was due
 Of sympathies.

She met a playmate, whose red rose
 Had never a thorn,
Whom fortune guided when she chose
 Her marriage morn,

And, smiling, looked her in the eye;
But, seeing the tears of sympathy,
Her smile died, and she passed on by
      In quiet scorn.

They could not know how, when by night
      The city slept,
A sleepless woman, still and white,
      The watches kept;
How her wife-loyal heart had borne
The keen pain of a flowerless thorn,
How hot the tears that smiles and scorn
      Had held unwept.

VISION

The wintry sun was pale
  On hill and hedge;
The wind smote with its flail
  The seeded sedge;
High up above the world,
  New taught to fly,
The withered leaves were hurled
  About the sky;
And there, through death and dearth,
  It went and came,—
The Glory of the earth
  That hath no name.

I know not what it is;
  I only know
It quivers in the bliss
  Where roses blow,
That on the winter's breath
  It broods in space,

And o'er the face of death
   I see its face,
And start and stand between
   Delight and dole,
As though mine eyes had seen
   A living Soul.

And I have followed it,
   As thou hast done,
Where April shadows flit
   Beneath the sun;
In dawn and dusk and star,
   In joy and fear,
Have seen its glory far
   And felt it near,
And dared recall his name
   Who stood unshod
Before a fireless flame,
   And called it God.

SEPTEMBER

I HAVE not been among the woods,
Nor seen the milk-weeds burst their hoods,

The downy thistle-seeds take wing,
Nor the squirrel at his garnering.

And yet I know that, up to God,
The mute month holds her goldenrod,

That clump and copse, o'errun with vines,
Twinkle with clustered muscadines,

And in deserted churchyard places
Dwarf apples smile with sunburnt faces.

I know how, ere her green is shed,
The dogwood pranks herself with red;

How the pale dawn, chilled through and
through,
Comes drenched and draggled with her dew;

How all day long the sunlight seems
As if it lit a land of dreams,

Till evening, with her mist and cloud,
Begins to weave her royal shroud.

If yet, as in old Homer's land,
Gods walk with mortals, hand in hand,

Somewhere to-day, in this sweet weather,
Thinkest thou not they walk together?

BAREFOOTED

THE girls all like to see the bluets in the lane
  And the saucy johnny-jump-ups in the
    meadow,
But, we boys, we want to see the dogwood
    blooms again,
  Throwin' a sort of summer-lookin' shadow;
For the very first mild mornin' when the woods
    are white
  (And we needn't even ask a soul about it)
We leave our shoes right where we pulled them
    off at night,
  And, barefooted once again, we run and
    shout it:
    You may take the country over—
    When the bluebird turns a rover,
    And the wind is soft and hazy,
    And you feel a little lazy,
    And the hunters quit the possums—
    It's the time for dogwood blossoms.

We feel so light we wish there were more fences
  here;
 We'd like to jump and jump them, all to-
  gether!
No sleds for us, no guns, nor even 'simmon beer,
 No nothin' but the blossoms and fair
  weather!
The meadow is a little sticky right at first,
 But a few short days 'll wipe away that
  trouble.
To feel so good and gay, I wouldn't mind the
  worst
 That could be done by any field o' stubble.
  O, all the trees are seemin' sappy!
  O, all the folks are smilin' happy!
 And there's joy in every little bit of room;
  But the happiest of them all
  At the Shanghai rooster's call
 Are we barefoots when the dogwoods burst
  abloom!

PARDON TIME

Give over now; forbear.   The moonlight steeps
In silver silence towered castle-keeps
  And cottage crofts, where apples bend the
      bough.
Peace guards us round, and many a tired heart
      sleeps.
  Let me brush back the shadow from your
      brow.
          Give over now.

On such a night, how sweet, how sweet is life,
Even to the insect piper with his fife!
  And must your troubled face still bear the
      blight
Of strength that runs itself to waste in strife?
  For love's own heart should throb through
      all the light
          Of such a night.

94

THE RATTLESNAKE

Coiled like a clod, his eyes the home of hate,
Where rich the harvest bows, he lies in wait,
Linking earth's death and music, mate with
    mate.

Is 't lure, or warning? Those small bells may
    sing
Like Ariel sirens, poised on viewless wing,
To lead stark life where mailéd death is king;

Else nature's voice, in that cold, earthy thrill,
Bids good avoid the venomed fang of ill,
And life and death fight equal in her will.

THE PRISONER

From pacing, pacing without hope or quest
He leaned against his window-bars to rest
And smelt the breeze that crept up from the
    west.

It came with sundown noises from the moors,
Of milking time and loud-voiced rural chores,
Of lumbering wagons and of closing doors.

He caught a whiff of furrowed upland sweet,
And certain scents stole up across the street
That told him fireflies winked among the wheat.

Over the dusk hill woke a new moon's light,
Shadowed the woods and made the waters white,
And watched above the quiet tents of night.

Alas, that the old Mother should not know
How ached his heart to be entreated so,
Who heard her calling and who could not go!

SONNET

To-day was but a dead day in my hands.
   Hour by hour did nothing more than pass,
   Mere idle winds above the faded grass.
And I, as though a captive held in bands,
Who, seeing a pageant, wonders much, but
          stands
   Apart, saw the sun blaze his course with brass
   And sink into his fabled sea of glass
With glory of farewell to many lands.

Thou knowest, thou who talliest life by days,
   That I have suffered more than pain of toil,
   Ah, more than they whose wounds are soothed
          with oil,
And they who see new light on beaten ways!
The prisoner I, who grasps his iron bars
And stares out into depth on depth of stars.

FOLK SONG

WHEN merry milkmaids to their cattle call
        At evenfall
        And voices range
Loud through the gloam from grange to quiet
     grange,

Wild waif-songs from long distant lands and
     loves,
        Like migrant doves,
        Wake and give wing
To passion dust-dumb lips were wont to sing.

The new still holds the old moon in her arms;
        The ancient charms
        Of dew and dusk
Still lure her nomad odors from the musk,

And, at each day's millennial eclipse,
        On new men's lips,
        Some old song starts,
Made of the music of millennial hearts,

Whereto one listens as from long ago
          And learns to know
          That one day's tears
And love and life are as a thousand years',

And that some simple shepherd, singing of
          His pain and love,
          May haply find
His heart-song speaks the heart of all his kind.

"97": THE FAST MAIL

Where the rails converge to the station yard
She stands one moment, breathing hard,

And then, with a snort and a clang of steel,
She settles her strength to the stubborn wheel,

And out, through the tracks that lead astray,
Cautiously, slowly she picks her way,

And gathers her muscle and guards her nerve,
When she swings her nose to the westward
    curve,

And takes the grade, which slopes to the sky,
With a bound of speed and a conquering cry.

The hazy horizon is all she sees,
Nor cares for the meadows, stirred with bees,

Nor the long, straight stretches of silent land,
Nor the ploughman, that shades his eye with
    his hand,

Nor the cots and hamlets that know no more
Than a shriek and a flash and a flying roar;

But, bearing her tidings, she trembles and
    throbs,
And laughs in her throat, and quivers and sobs;

And the fire in her heart is a red core of heat,
That drives like a passion through forest and
    street,

Till she sees the ships in their harbor at rest,
And sniffs at the trail to the end of her quest.

If I were the driver who handles her reins,
Up hill and down hill and over the plains,

To watch the slow mountains give back in the
    west,
To know the new reaches that wait every crest,

To hold, when she swerves, with a confident
    clutch,
And feel how she shivers and springs to the
    touch,

With the snow on her back and the sun in her
    face,
And nothing but time as a quarry to chase,

101

I should grip hard my teeth, and look where she
    led,
And brace myself stooping, and give her her
    head,

And urge her, and soothe her, and serve all her
    need,
And exult in the thunder and thrill of her speed.

SUNDOWN

HILLS, wrapped in gray, standing along the
    west;
  Clouds, dimly lighted, gathering slowly;
The star of peace at watch above the crest—
  Oh, holy, holy, holy!

We know, O Lord, so little what is best;
  Wingless, we move so lowly;
But in thy calm all-knowledge let us rest—
  Oh, holy, holy, holy!

AT SEA

When the dim, tall sails of the ships were in
    motion,
  Ghostly, and slow, and silent-shod,
We gazed where the dusk fled over the ocean,
  A great gray hush, like the shadow of God.

The sky dome cut with its compass in sunder
  A circle of sea from the darkened land,—
A circle of tremulous waste and wonder,
  O'er which one groped with a childish hand.

The true stars came to their stations in heaven,
  The false stars shivered deep down in the sea,
And the white crests went like monsters, driven
  By winds that never would let them be,

And there, where the elements mingled and
    muttered,
  We stood, each man with a lone dumb heart,
Full of the vastness that never was uttered
  By symbol of words or by echo of art.

L'ENVOI

GOD willed, who never needed speech,
    "Let all things be:"
And, lo, the starry firmament
    And land and sea
And his first thought of life that lives
      In you and me.

His circle of eternity
    We see in part;
Our spirits are his breath, our hearts
    Beat from his heart;
Hence we have played as little gods
    And called it art.

Lacking his power, we shared his dream
    Of perfect things;
Between the tents of hope and sweet
    Rememberings
Have sat in ashes, but our souls
    Went forth on wings.

Where life fell short of some desire
    In you and me,
Feeling for beauty which our eyes
    Could never see,
Behold, from out the void we willed
    That it should be,

And sometimes dreamed our lisping songs
    Of humanhood
Might voice his silent harmony
    Of waste and wood,
And he, beholding his and ours,
    Might find it good.